Israel at 40

Years of Triumphs, Trials & Errors

Covers Events from 1983 through 1987

An American Cartoonist's View of Israel

by Noah Bee

Foreword by Wolf Blitzer

BLOCH PUBLISHING CO.

Copyright © 1988 by Noah Bee

All rights reserved. No part of this book may be reproduced in any manner whatsoever without the written permission of the author or publisher.

Published by Bloch Publishing Co Inc.
Manufactured in the United States of America.

Library of Congress Cataloging-in-Publication Data

Bee, Noah.
   Years of triumphs, trials & errors.

   "Covers events from 1983 through 1987."
   1. Israel--Politics and government--Caricatures and cartoons. I. Title. II. Title: Years of triumphs, trials, and errors.
DS126.5.B332   1988   956.94'054'0207   88-7336
ISBN 0-8197-0555-1

*To David, Aliza, Elisabeth and Gidon
for the joy of watching them grow*

Acknowledgements

When my last book "The Impossible Takes A Little Longer" was published in 1983, our grandson David asked me if I would dedicate my book to the youngest generation. So the idea was born and with the upcoming 40th anniversary of the State of Israel this was an appropriate occasion to fulfill his wish.

May I take this opportunity to express my deep gratitude to Wolf Blitzer, the Washington Bureau Chief of the "Jerusalem Post" who wrote the Foreword for this volume. His keen mind and knowledge of the Israeli and American Jewish scenes makes him the most authoritative spokesman on these subjects. Thanks, Wolf, for your kind words.

Ever since Murray Zuckoff became editor-in-chief of the Jewish Telegraphic Agency we worked together to make sure that the cartoons which appeared over a week after our conversation were still timely. So it was natural that he agreed to edit the sequence of events and write the captions.

It was also Ted Sandler, the editor of "Israel Today" where a large number of my cartoons had appeared who helped me with his good judgment and added his talents in writing the last captions of the book.

I wish to mention my dear friends, Ernest Barbarash and David Horowitz who were always available with good advice and assistance in getting some historical facts straight.

It is good to be related to the renowned photographer Arthur Lavine, who made me look good.

Above all loving kudos to my wife Marian who patiently corrected my spelling and did all of the typing. She more than anyone else helped in making this volume a reality.

Foreword

As a youngster growing up in Buffalo, New York, I became an avid reader of the local Jewish newspaper, the "Jewish Review." It arrived in the mail every Friday. I was usually the first in my family to grab it. I had become fascinated with Israel in 1961—the year my parents took me to Israel to celebrate my Bar Mitzvah. Like Israel, I was born in 1948. Upon my return from that first visit to Israel, I knew that I would have to stay in touch with the country. The "Jewish Review" was one way.

And reading that paper resulted in my becoming familiar with the cartoons of Noah Bee. In fact, I often turned the pages to his weekly contribution first thing. It is fair to say that over the years, I have become one of his great fans. I have continued to scan the weekly Jewish newspapers in the United States to gain his insights in the latest twists and turns of the Jewish people, especially those in Israel. He has never disappointed me.

It took many years before I first met Noah Bee. But I felt that I already knew him well. Many of his cartoons were permanently etched in my mind. He certainly influenced my thinking, as he no doubt did to many others as well.

With a few bold or soft strokes, he could capture the essence of an event unfolding in Israel or in Jewish communities around the world. This became even more apparent to me when I became a professional journalist. I, of course, was deeply involved in covering a story—whether Sadat's trip to Jerusalem or the war in Lebanon or the Pollard spy scandal or the most recent riots on the West Bank and Gaza Strip. I was busy writing words to try to make some sense out of these events. I struggled to prepare a 2,000 word article. But Noah Bee, very often, could make that very same point better with only one drawing and a handful of words. I delighted in his talent and wisdom.

Political cartoons are an essential part of journalism. Every good newspaper must publish them; their readers demand it. The Jewish press in the United States and Canada has been blessed over the years to have access to Noah Bee's work, especially at a time when so many of the popular cartoonists in the general press are having a field day in lambasting Israel. Noah Bee's sensitivity and caring for Israel and the Jewish people stand in marked contrast. Even when he is critical—as is his right—it is obvious that he is moved by a basic love for his people. His weekly cartoons are a testimony to that love.

Readers of this book will be moved to laugh, to cry and to think. They will recall the most recent story of the Jewish People—a continuing saga. The challenge remains. There is no shortage of problems. This book—like Noah Bee's previous ones—helps to keep that struggle in perspective. And for that, I am grateful.

Washington, D.C.　　　　　　　　　　　　　　　　　　　　　　　　Wolf Blitzer
February 26, 1988

Introduction

T imes of crises or unique historic events are the essential ingredients which move a political cartoonist to creative heights. It has been my fortune that in doing cartoons on the subject of Israel ever since its creation, there has not been a single dull moment nor a dearth of ideas. Who could foresee that at its beginning the infant State would withstand the onslaught of seven Arab armies, defeat them, build a nation in every sense of the word with a powerful army. And who could have foreseen the Six Day blitz that astounded the entire world. Or Nasser's successor setting foot in Jerusalem and making peace with its arch enemy. The cartoonist's lot is a constant journey between today's harsh realities and the anticipation of tomorrow's developments. He has to be able to analyze the nuances and complexities of a constantly changing reality and to be able to abstract what is essential and relatively permanent in events that are for the most part ephemeral or only partially emergent.

Looking over my cartoons about the Middle East that I drew 40 or 10 years ago, I find that many of them could have been drawn today. True the map of the region has changed, endless upheavals and revolutions have taken place, governments have come and gone. Thousands of human beings have been killed and scores assassinated, but truly very little has changed in the minds and the behavior of the people. The same suspicions, mistrust and unwillingness to compromise in a peaceful manner still persists as it did 40 years ago.

It is with mixed emotions that we remember the world of yesteryear. It seems that

only recently the Allied nations rejoiced on their victory over Hitler. Unfortunately there are still would be Hitlers and Neo-Nazi ideologies that try to raise their head and once again threaten the democratic world. Looking closer at the map one can hardly identify all of the new countries which have sprung up as a result of the breakup of old empires and the emergence of new ones like the Soviet Union. In 1945 when the United Nations was established there were 34 member-nations. Today, in 1987 the number has grown to 158. We are living in an undulating world where time and space chase each other in remorseless cycles.

Walking in New York City's Rockefeller Center or at the U.N. Plaza on the East River, one cannot help but notice the sea of flags with the entire spectrum of colors and symbols that are fluttering in the New York air. There are big countries, medium countries, small countries and even mini countries. They all gather in that coffin shaped glass skyscraper on the East River and they form what Marshall McLuhan called "the global village." Each one tries to advance its own interests. Mostly, however, it is not the size of the country that gets attention, but its strategic importance to where the two superpowers have a foothold or exert influence. One such country is a small piece of real estate called Israel. Wedged in between the crossroads of Asia and Africa and surrounded on three sides by a sea of the Moslem Nations, it stands out like a beacon casting a light of historic, religious and strategic importance. Since time immemorial, this land called Eretz Yisrael or Palestine has had the misfortune to be in the center of an untold number of conflicts and invasions. It took almost 2,000 years of exile for the original inhabitants to return to this place, because it was the only land they could call their own.

Since my early youth I was interested in politics, so it was natural that I turned my talent in this direction. Growing up in Palestine in the 1930's I experienced the molding of a new society which laid the foundation for the future Jewish State. It was my luck that I got a break and had my first cartoons published at the age of 17. I contributed to various publications, ultimately doing cartoons for the "Palestine Post" which later changed its name to "Jerusalem Post." After coming to the U.S. during World War II I got a better perspective of Jewish problems in and out of Palestine. These were the days when we learned about the Holocaust and I felt that I should channel my ideas and endeavors to subjects closest to my heart; that of Jewish safety and the survival of our people. The struggle to open the gates of Palestine for the remnants of the Holocaust became the paramount priority for the American Jews. Leading in this campaign were the Zionist groups, the largest among them being the Zionist Organization of America. My first cartoons appeared in their official publication, "American Zionist" where several of my cartoons were printed in each issue.

In 1959, I was offered an opportunity to do a weekly cartoon for the Jewish Telegraphic Agency Syndicate, which disseminates news to most of the Jewish press in this country and abroad. Almost 30 years have gone by and I still hammer out my weekly cartoon.

It was the Balfour Declaration which laid the foundation for the establishment of a Jewish National Home in Palestine. This in turn sparked a nationalistic awakening of its Arab population, but in spite of this the period between WWI and WWII

witnessed a steady increase in the Jewish population coupled with an unprecedented economic and political development. Jewish ingenuity, capital, and idealism established an oasis in this neglected and parched land. Zionism was giving birth to a different kind of Jew. It created collectives, labor unions and it established a new society, a society that had its roots in the nationalist and socialist ideologies of Europe of the 19th Century. Because of these new opportunities, Arabs from neighboring countries started streaming into Palestine, also, thereby increasing the local population by two or three times its original size.

May 15, 1948 marks the culmination of the Zionist dream. On that day David Ben-Gurion proclaimed the birth of the State of Israel. Ever since that day the State became the center of the Middle East conflict and its importance grew constantly in the face of Arab hostility.

The Six Day War established Israel as the dominant regional power. It became the high point of the nation's existence—it's finest hour. With Jerusalem in Israeli hands the prayers of the millenia became a reality. The city was finally united.

However, the price of victory was two sided. It raised the hope for peace but added a burden of 800,000 additional Arabs in the newly acquired territories. But when the Arabs rejected peace offers by the victors, it became clear that nothing had changed in the Arab mind, except the map. Shlomo Avinari, a leading Israeli theorist recalls Golda Meir saying at that time, "we can wait a few months, a year or maybe more, they will come around" but nothing happened. On the other hand, things began to change in Israel. After two millenia, many saw the fulfillment of a dream. Now the biblical Judea and Samaria were in Jewish hands.

If no peace could be achieved, then what the alternative? From the beginning of practical Zionism the early pioneers believed that the way to establish permanency was to create facts. This was an old pioneering credo of the Zionists. So the idea of settling the newly acquired territories gained momentum.

With the new borders, the country entered a period of a fool's paradise. A sense of complacency set in, but did not last for long. The Yom Kippur War hit Israel in its solar plexis. It was caught completely off guard. It took a few days to awaken the nation to the full impact of the tragedy. As twice before, Israelis rose to the challenge and carried the war to the gates of Damascus and on the road to Cairo, but with great human losses. The effect of those trying days left a scar on the country and its politics. It weakened the Labor Government, which was held responsible for the state of unpreparedness. Each leader, in turn, but specifically, Defense Minister Moshe Dayan, was excoriated by the public.

While the American people were celebrating their bicentennial on July 4, 1976, Israel surprised the world with its historic rescue at Entebbe. It underscored the resolve and ability to deal with terrorists.

The psychological trauma of the Yom Kippur War and breaking scandals within the Labor Party produced in the 1977 elections unprecedented results. For the first time since the establishment of the State the Labor coalition lost. The country took a 360° turn. The ascent of Menachem Begin to Premiership after all the years of disregard and ridicule brought new policies and new faces to the surface. The Labor Party found itself in disarray and tried to pick up the pieces. Begin proved to be an excellent politician. He included in his Cabinet people of different ideologies

13

like Moshe Dayan, hero of the Six Day War and the former chief of staff and famed archeologist, Yigal Yadin.

But the most dramatic event came from the least expected source when President Anwar Sadat, to the amazement of the entire world, set foot in Jerusalem carrying an olive branch. This was followed by a period of great expectations and exhilaration in Israel. The whole world watched on TV in amazement when the two antagonists Begin and Sadat sat down on the lawn of the White House and signed a peace accord known as the "Camp David Agreement". It soon became clear that the bone of contention was the interpretation of the agreement.

Relative peace followed but international charades continued. President Carter and the West European bloc tried to include the PLO terrorists as a part of the peace process. The Venice meeting of the European Economic Community extended recognition to the PLO as the legitimate representative of the Palestinian people. Arafat was riding high but it did not get him anywhere.

The United States had a giant problem on its hands. In 1979 the world was shaken when the Shah of Iran was overthrown and a fanatical regime seized power in Iran. The new ruler Ayatolla Khomeini, declared Israel as one of its main enemies and embraced the PLO.

A new American President was elected in 1980. Coming after Carter who was promoting a "Palestinian Homeland" with the participation of the PLO, Reagan's election victory was a welcome relief. He was considered a friend of Israel.

In June, 1981, Israel in an act of sheer chutzpah bombed and destroyed the Iraqi nuclear reactor near Baghdad and in October the world was stunned by the assassination of President Anwar Sadat by Moslem fanatics. In spite of these two incidents the peace process continued, but as soon as Egypt recovered the Sinai, peace became a one-way street.

After the new elections in Israel in 1981 something important was brewing in the closed sessions of the government. Tired and provoked by constant shelling of its northern towns by the PLO, Israel was making plans to get rid of this nuisance once and for all. From the time the civil war broke out in Lebanon in the early 70's, the PLO was accumulating arms and men and became a state within a state there.

On June 6, 1982 "Operation Peace For the Galilee" was launched. This operation which was supposed to last a few days stretched to almost three years and hung over the nation's neck like an albatross. The cost in terms of lives was tremendous with a terrible drain on its economy and saw the resignation of Menachem Begin. What was supposed to be a cleaning up of the PLO plague from the border area, became a chase to the gates of Beirut. The architect of it all, Ariel Sharon intended to trap Arafat and the PLO infrastructure and once and for all put an end to the constant shelling of its northern frontier. Militarily it succeeded but politically it was a disaster. Israel's ally, the leader of the Marionite Christians, Bashir Gemayel was elected President of Lebanon. A few days later he was assassinated. The cooperation between the Christians and Israel began to fall apart. With the new situation, Israel evacuated the positions near Beirut. That was followed by the terrible

massacre of Palestinians in the refugee camps of Sabra and Shatila. The world was shocked to see on TV the scenes of dead bodies of women and children. The media pointed the finger at Israel. Israel, always vulnerable to world opinion, was staggered by the development. All of its enemies came out of the woodwork and labeled it an aggressor. A certain amount of the blame has to be shared by the Israeli press and some of its commentators. They were not only outspoken, but flaggelated the government and each other. But under a groundswell of public pressure a committee was established to inquire into the tragedy at the refugee camps.

In all of this turmoil, President Reagan dispatched a contingent of Marines to Beirut with the intention of restoring order, but as it turned out it only saved Arafat and the PLO from total destruction and helped evacuate them to different parts of the Arab world.

New elections in Israel produced a deadlock and after lengthy negotiations the two largest parties, Likud and Labor formed a national unity government that would rotate leadership every two years. The priority of the new government was to pull the Israeli forces out of Lebanon. This has been an ideal period for a cartoonist. It gave birth to twins who are on the opposite sides of the political pole, whose social philosophies contradict each other but out of "Ain Breirah" carry on the affairs of the State on the basis of rotation. Upon this decision the first Premiership went to Shimon Peres of Labor-Alignment. He successfully pulled the Israeli forces out of Lebanon and handed over the whole mess to the Syrians.

When the withdrawal was completed in the Spring of 1985, the domestic stove

began to overheat. The Israeli pressure cooker was boiling over with problems that had been swept under the carpet for a long time.

Ever since the Six Day War with the addition of new territories and new borders, a new psychological reality developed. Various cultural and religious groups began to compete with each other for a greater share in the national pie. The shift from the Ashkenazic majority to the Sephardic changed the character of Zionism and the society. The 1977 election forged an alliance between the Revisionist Herut, the Sephardic community and religious groups formed a Likud coalition. A new drive was launched to create more settlements, spearheaded by religious elements. These religious young people rejected the pragmatic and moderating policies of the Labor Party and took the lead in settling the biblical frontiers. At present there are 140,000 Jews living in 114 cities and settlements.

A new phenomena appeared on the horizon: American born Rabbi Meir Kahane was preaching expulsion of all Arabs to Jordan. With the territories in Israeli hands, the Arab population benefited economically. Their standard of living rose greatly. Nevertheless their sympathies toward the PLO increased. The government tried to find leaders among the local Arabs who would cooperate in self-rule but those who did were assassinated. Few were willing to take the risk under the circumstances. Miron Benvenisti, the former vice mayor of Jerusalem maintains that the settlement structure has become permanent and is irreversible. King Hussein fearing the worst tried to sit down and negotiate for peace with Israel. To accomplish this he needed the cooperation of the PLO, but after lengthy discussions with Arafat, the plan fell through.

In the meantime, the pressure cooker was getting closer to exploding. Inflation reached 800%. Ultra orthodox religious groups became more strident and demanding. They tried to have the Knesset enact archaic laws on the country around the issue of who is a Jew to a point of calling for the amendment of the Law of Return. This ongoing effort has threatened to alienate the major segment of American Jewry.

A new move for an international conference on Middle East peace under the auspices of the U.N. Security Council is currently deadlocked. This turned into a contest between Shimon Peres who is pushing for it and Itzhak Shamir who opposes it.

This volume deals with events of the past five years, from 1983 to 1988. My first book "In Spite of Everything" covered the first 25 years of the State. The second "The Impossible Takes a Little Longer" dealt with the following years between 1973 to 1983, so it was natural that I would follow it up with a third volume in Israel's 40th anniversary year.

This period was dominated by the end of the Lebanese nightmare, the Pollard spy case, the Irangate scandal, problems with Mossad and endless internal discords. For a cartoonist, it was like getting shots of adrenalin.

The most serious problem confronting the country today is that of emigration or yerida. The foundation of the Zionist dream was based on the concept of Aliyah in gathering, so this disturbing development is the most challenging of the present or any future government.

It was President Truman who rushed to recognize the newly established State, so it was obvious that a close relationship would develop between the two countries. Bound by a large and influential U.S. Jewish community, the Biblical sentiments and strategic importance, it was very natural that Israel should be counted as one of America's strongest supporters. No other country has such a pro-United States voting record in the U.N. as Israel. As a result of the Six Day War the USSR and its satellites, except Rumania severed their ties with Israel, so the country had to put all of its eggs into one basket. With the Arabs constantly playing both sides, it became obvious that only Israel could be a reliable ally in the region. This reality puts Israel in a "Catch-22" position. It wants to retain the strong support of the U.S. and at the same time it would like to renew its diplomatic relations with the Soviets in order to develop a more independent foreign policy. Only time will tell if they will be successful.

Now with Israel's forthcoming 40th anniversary I have highlighted on top of these pages the outstanding moments in its history. In terms of Jewish history this is a short span of time, but in an age when time travels faster than sound, the events have had volcanic repercussions.

Jewish history is full of miracles and Israel has had more than a fair share of them. Miracles have been the story of the Jewish existence but in Israel everybody takes them for granted. The number 40 symbolizes one of them. The 40 years of wandering in the desert, as the story goes for the slave generation to die out so that only free men would enter the Promised Land. Israel of today has not been quite that

19

way. The desert generation has become a generation that has succeeded in converting the arid land into a blooming garden. It took a hounded and uprooted people of the Shtetl and Casbah and transformed them into free people in a sovereign place filled with dignity, pride and gave birth to a fighting Jew.

The winds of Shiite fundamentalism hangs over the entire region. Now is the time for the moderate Arabs to come to their senses and realize who is the true enemy of stability and progress. But alas this is the Middle East and paraphrasing Winston Churchill "It is a riddle wrapped in a mystery inside an enigma."

As the country and world Jewry began to celebrate the milestone anniversary serious riots broke out in Gaza and spread to the West Bank. Faced with an open rebellion by stones and fire bombs, Israel had to adopt a strong arm policy to restore law and order. For a democratic society these were hard and agonizing choices. Israel is paying a high price in world opinion and even among some American-Jewish leaders. As of this moment it is not clear when all of this will end. Hopefully, out of the anger and rage some semblance of sanity can emerge and like Esau and Jacob in the days of old, who after a lifelong hate for each other made peace; so too, peace can be achieved in this tormented land.

In facing the future one has to look at the past to be able to make sense of it all. The philosopher George Santayana put it this way, "Those who do not remember the past are condemned to relive it." So it is my hope that the Israeli leaders of today and tomorrow will not forget this for the single purpose of justifying the Jewish existence and its survival.

Noah Bee

1983

The Burden of Lebanon

Reagan's Peace Plan

Begin's Resignation

Rise of Shamir

President Hosni Mubarak of Egypt balks at implementing the provisions of the Camp David agreement once Israel has returned the Sinai peninsula with its oilfields and air force bases to Egypt, an element of the Camp David accord that had been agreed to by Israeli Prime Minister Menachem Begin and then Egyptian President Anwar Sadat.

Aghast at the massacre of Palestinian refugees at the Sabra and Shatila camps in Beirut by Christian Phalangists, Israel set up a commission of inquiry into this tragedy. The focus is on then Defense Minister Ariel Sharon who resigns after he is found culpable in the massacre.

The U.S. government tries to get the Israel Defense forces out of the security zone in south Lebanon which serves as a buffer between Israel and Lebanon.

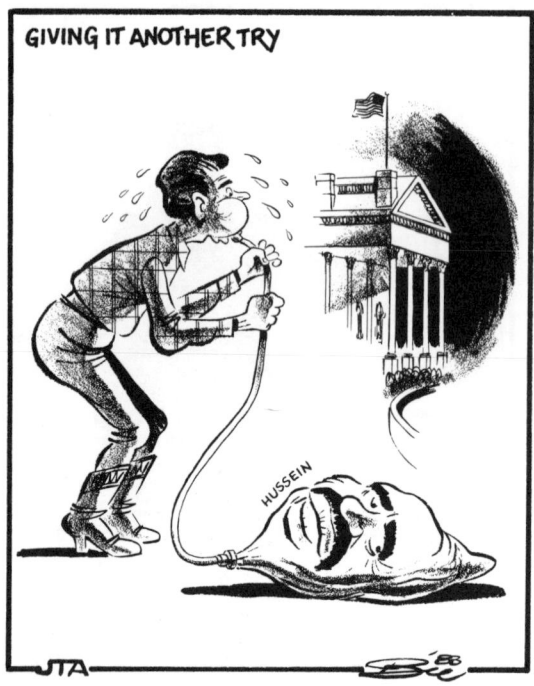

President Reagan tries to breathe life into his contention that King Hussein of Jordan is capable of playing a viable role in achieving Middle East peace.

With the increase of Israeli settlements on the West Bank, time is running out for an Arab autonomy plan.

Reagan devises a plan to bring the Israelis and the Jordanians together to end hostilities and start negotiating for peace, but there are no takers.

U.S. Secretary of State George Shultz goes to the Middle East in order to implement Reagan's peace plan but expresses particular interest in pressuring Israel to be more forthcoming.

President Hafez Assad of Syria rejects Shultz's endeavor to bring him into the peace process, but Shultz refuses to write off the Syrian leader.

Reagan, beguiled by his own Alice-in-Wonderland Middle East policies, tries to decide on an ad hoc basis whether Israel should remain as the U.S. surrogate in the quagmire of Lebanon's civil war.

Palestine Liberation Organization chairman Yasir Arafat is looking for a political safety net to avoid the pitfall of being isolated and crushed by the internecine warfare of PLO's warring camps.

The Soviet Union continues to arm Assad as he steps up threats against Israel. The Soviets believe that a friendly Syria would provide them with a foothold in the Middle East.

In spite of the obvious obstacles the Soviet Union and Syria place on the road to peace, Reagan blithely continues to act as if smiles and slogans can soften the harsh realities of the Arab-Israeli conflict.

28

Officially sanctioned and unofficially, anti-Semitism continues to be brewed in the Soviet cauldron of government pronouncements and in outpourings in sundry publications.

Arafat, beset by warring factions in his organization, becomes the object of Assad's wrath and ridicule who refuses to recognize him as the sole legitimate representative of the Palestinian people. A dissident PLO faction which emerged after Arafat fled from Lebanon has won the support of Assad.

Robert McFarlane, Assistant Secretary of State, makes an effort to win Assad over to Reagan's peace plan but has no more success than his two predecessors in a similar mission, Secretary of State Shultz and Reagan's special envoy to the Mideast, Philip Habib.

Egypt is holding back reestablishment of full diplomatic relations with the Jewish State in order to build up their prestige in the Arab world.

Prime Minister Menachem Begin, who sought for nearly 30 years to become Israel's leader and finally succeeded in 1977, leaves office after a series of remarkable achievements. His departure before his term of office ended was prompted by the debacle in Lebanon and the death of his wife Aliza.

Yitzhak Shamir, a leader of the Herut faction in the Likud coalition, replaces Begin as Israel's Premier and faces enormous problems of inflation, social tensions, political dissent, political infighting in Likud, unrest in the West Bank and continued hostility by the Arab world, except Egypt.

Assad is suspected as the triggerman behind the massacre of American and French troops in the peacekeeping force in Lebanon.

The U.S. and USSR, each in its own way and for its own reasons, try to save Arafat from defeat by the warring Palestinian factions. Essentially, the PLO leader appears to act as a buffer between the Palestinian moderates and extremists.

The PLO is held responsible for arming young Palestinian anti-Israeli protestors in the West Bank.

Reagan has little faith that President Pierre Gemayal of Lebanon is capable of persuading Assad to end his military intervention in Lebanon but to use diplomatic influence instead, to help bring peace to the war-torn country.

* MAY IT BE KHOMEINI'S, SYRIAN, PLO'S OR ANY OTHER

The Reagan Administration seems befuddled about the origin of Arab terrorism, its nature, objective and consequences, and fails to take appropriate steps to curb it.

Jesse Jackson, a Democratic Party presidential hopeful, visits the Mideast and meets with Arafat. Their embrace is felt around the world. American Jews and Israelis are aghast at this development and denounce the meeting.

Premier Yitzhak Shamir of Israel is trying to curb the skyrocketing inflation and in cushioning the tensions and conflicts engendered by the situation.

1984

Labor and Likud

Form a Government

of National Unity.

Peres takes over the Reins

Ethiopian Exodus

Israel is contemplating being cast in
the role as the American quartermaster
in the Mideast.

HAPPINESS IS...

Soon after Arafat expressed delight in the assassination of Sadat, President Mubarak received the PLO chieftain.

THE JOKER IS WILD

Jackson is again in the public limelight as he goes to the Mideast to meet with Assad, bypassing official diplomatic efforts by the U.S. to deal with the Syrian leader.

All kinds of statements are being made by Egyptian officials and the Egyptian press that once they recovered the land, the Camp David Agreement is not valid anymore.

The Lebanese, hit by civil war fomented by the PLO, at first welcomed the Israeli Defense Force as liberators, but then sought to solve their problem with the aid of American or Syrian troops. However, subsequent events forced the U.S. to withdraw its peacekeeping troops and provided the rationale for the entrenchment of Syrian troops in the Bekaa valley.

King Hussein is hesitant about negotiating with Israel as long as the PLO demands that it play a role as a partner with Jordan in the negotiations.

THE DIGGER AND THE MOURNER

HERE RESTS LEBANON — A VICTIM OF TERROR AND DOUBLE-CROSS

DEMOCRACY

Assad seals Lebanon's doom by stationing Syrian troops in the Bekaa valley region and exacerbating tensions and hostilities between Lebanese Christians and Moslems.

FISHING SEASON ON THE NILE

ISLAMIC CONFERENCE

Egypt is trying to return to the Arab fold through the Islamic conference by supporting the PLO.

MILKING THE UNMILKABLE

The Reagan Administration, ignoring reality, continues to woo the PLO in the naive hope that it can achieve a new look and thus make it a palatable element in Mideast peace negotiations.

Syria replaces the PLO as the force manipulating the various factions in Lebanon and making certain that they remain divided and dependent on Syria to act as an intermediary and peacemaker.

In an effort to wrest military concessions from the U.S., Saudi Arabia presents itself as the leading contender for implementing the American peace plan in the Mideast.

WILL THE REAL PALESTINIAN STAND UP!

The initial issue had been who represents the Palestinian people. But the question that gradually emerged was who controls those who claim to speak for the Palestinians.

King Hussein rejects as an insult an American arms deal as too little and threatens to buy arms elsewhere.

Israeli politicians Ezer Weizman, Yitzhak Shamir and Shimon Peres flex their political muscles as another round of national elections begins.

A DIFFERENT BRANCH

The PLO, forced to flee from Lebanon where it had found a safe perch, finds another safe haven in Syria from where they can launch terrorist actions against Israel.

One of the most contentious problems in Israel is the Orthodox Rabbinate's insistence that conversions to Judaism are not valid if performed by Conservative or Reform rabbis. The Orthodox rabbis and the Orthodox Members of Knesset are campaigning to amend the Law of Return to include a clause that only those conversions done according to halacha (Jewish law) would be recognized.

During the American election campaign, presidential contenders Gary Hart and Mondale are trying to woo Jewish voters, while Jesse Jackson is dancing to a different tune.

While the Arab world around Israel is full of warfare, intrigue, assassinations and the call for Jihad, Israel is exercising its democratic duty by preparing for elections.

HIS TRIPS AND HIS SKIPS

Pope John Paul II tours the Middle East to spread his message of piety and peace but carefully avoids including Israel in his itinerary.

The Reagan Administration can't seem to focus in on the PLO as the basic intransigent enemy of the State of Israel, and searches instead for other nebulous and obscure culprits.

LOOKING FOR TERRORISTS

The outcome of Israel's elections is monitored carefully by Arab leaders anxious to determine what next steps to take against the Jewish State and how to justify their actions to the Western world.

Washington and Saudi Arabia find that they have a great deal in common, especially defending investments in each other's country. A united front on the issue of Mideast peace would benefit both, and Israel could in the process be left out in the cold.

GULLIVERS AMONG LILLIPUTS

Two largest parties, Likud and Labor, are being hamstrung by blackmail demands of little splinter parties.

THE ERASER

Continuing PLO terror provides ever-greater evidence that it does not represent the genuine interests and aspirations of the Palestinian people.

Rabbi Meir Kahane, the leader of the
Kach Party and its representative in the
Knesset, is hurting Israel by his virulent
anti-Arab views and his demand for the
expulsion of all Arabs from Israel.

Yigal Yadin, a veteran Zionist whose archaeological discoveries illuminated the Biblical past, and a founder of the State of Israel, died in 1984 at the age of 68.

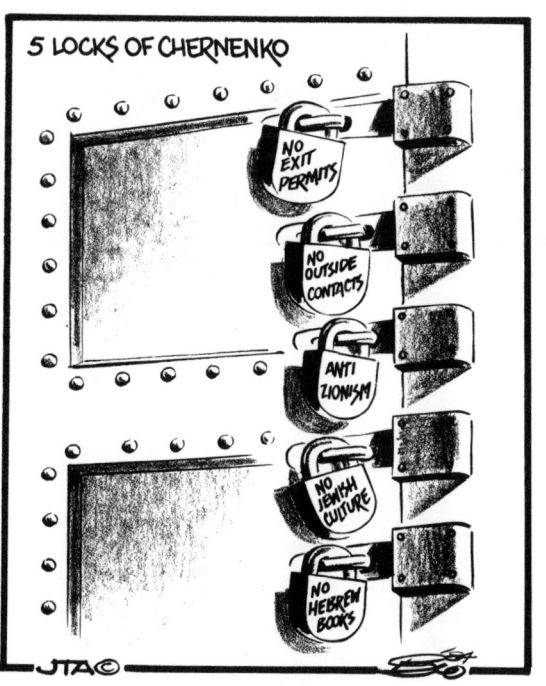

Soviet leader Andrei Chernenko clamps down on Jews in the USSR by imposing stringent restrictions on their quest for emigration and the study and propagation of Jewish culture.

Mubarak, seized with doubts about the efficacy of Camp David signed by his predecessor, President Anwar Sadat, invites the Russians back into Egypt after they were tossed out by Sadat in the early 1970's.

Israel's democracy is fragmented and paralyzed by the profusion of some 20 splinter parties which demand a place in the country's political sun despite their marginal role in the real political arena.

The U.S. Senate subcommittee dawdles on the issue of agreeing to approve legislation for a free trade zone for Israel. The establishment of such a zone, which would lower tariffs for Israeli goods sold in the U.S., was approved by U.S. economic experts in talks with their Israeli counterparts.

Israel is besieged simultaneously by domestic politics, religious extremism, economic eruptions, enemies from abroad and by ongoing Arab hostility towards the Jewish State.

The Soviet-Arab-Third World knaves that cohabit in the United Nations try to devise ways of isolating Israel in the world body in order to divert attention away from the human rights violations in their own countries.

A new government of national unity emerges in Israel after a prolonged period of voting, political maneuvering and parliamentary bickering.

But despite the unity government of Labor leader Shimon Peres and Likud leader Yitzhak Shamir, divergences and antagonisms continue on basic policy issues.

The problems that emerged under the previous Likud government continue to plague the unity government which must assume responsibility for past neglect and excesses.

Peres' first function as Prime Minister is to tackle the enormous inflation that prevails in Israel.

Mubarak and Hussein seek to forge an alliance that would exclude Israel from a pivotal role in determining the future status of the West Bank and sidestep the Camp David accords which spell out the elements of autonomy for the West Bank.

ISRAEL'S HELL'S ANGEL

Kahane's extreme views are alien to the Israeli political scene. He is depicted as an oddball and is condemned by the Israeli public.

The U.S. and France, both striving to maintain a foothold in the Mideast, woo the Arabs with promises of delivering advanced military arms.

ANYTHING YOU CAN DO I CAN DO BETTER

RAPID FORCE FOR JORDAN — 4 BILLION ARMS FOR SAUDIS

MITTERRAND

Israel hopes the United States will get its message for additional badly needed economic aid in fighting the enormous inflation by cutting the red tape.

THE BEAR HUG

AMMAN PLO / DAMASCUS PLO

The Soviet Union, which seeks a united terrorist front against Israel, urges each side of the squabbling PLO to find common ground against a common enemy and pledges to support a unified PLO.

The unity government's austerity program—a move calculated to curb soaring inflation—has a chilling effect on the Israeli public, which finds itself with a scarcity of consumer goods.

Shimon, it's cold inside

AUSTERITY

MADE IN ISRAEL

THE CRY OF THE FALASHA

ORTHODOX JEWRY

ORGANIZED JEWISH COMMUNITY

The endangered Jews of Ethiopia plead with world Jewry to save them, but the Orthodox Jews who question their Jewishness and the established Jewish community leadership which questions the expediency of financing their freedom tune out the cries for help.

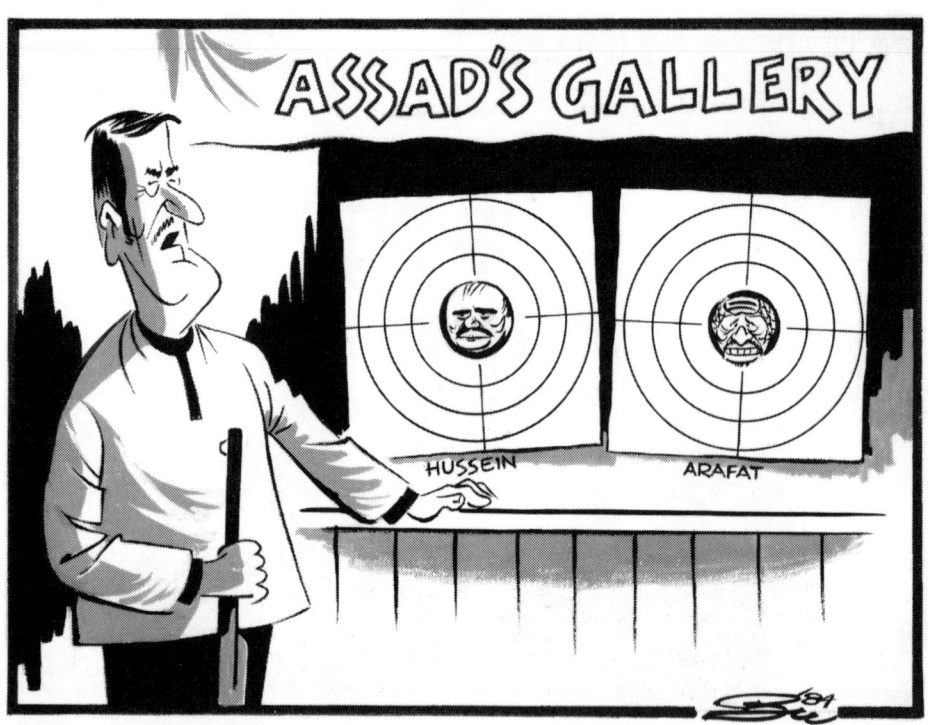

Assad would like to attain the leadership of the Palestinian people by eliminating Hussein and Arafat as competitors for this role.

Both presidential aspirants, Reagan and Mondale, as is customary, are trying to woo the Jewish voters by their pro-Israeli statements.

It is hard for Peres to negotiate an evacuation plan with Lebanon, which is manipulated completely by Assad.

Arafat, suffering a series of major setbacks beginning with his flight from Lebanon, insists that he is nevertheless still the leader of the Palestinian people.

The unity government of Labor and Likud is a historically ironic formation. The Labor Party once headed by David Ben Gurion and the Herut party, a faction in the Likud coalition, once led by Zeev Jabotinsky, were implacable enemies during their lifetimes.

Israel's intentions for direct talks about the plight of the Palestinian people in the West Bank evokes negative responses from Palestinian representatives, Jordan and Egypt calculated to frustrate and derail this objective.

1985

Exit from Lebanon

Reagan goes to Bitburg

Who is a Jew

Kahane Phenomenon

Israel, in a series of daring and dangerous airlifts, rescues some 10,000 Black Ethiopian Jews in what is dubbed "Operation Moses," giving lie to those who contended that Israel was indifferent to the plight of the Ethiopian Jews and to those who defamed Zionism as a form of racism.

Secretary of State George Shultz urges the Israeli government to continue its austerity policy if it wants to continue receiving economic aid from the U.S., a move decried by Israelis and American Jews as an unwarranted interference in Israel's internal policies.

GEORGE P. SHULTZ

Dear Shimon,

Three cheers for your first 100 days. The U.S. government is with you all the way. Keep up the good work.

yours,
George

P.S. Attached you'll find a belt. Keep on tightening it!

POT CALLING KETTLE BLACK

You Zionist Agent!

You Zionist Lover!

Two archenemies of Israel, Assad and Arafat, are trying to outdo each other in their hostility towards the Jewish State and Zionism.

HUSSEIN THE SWINGER

Jordan's monarch, in a game of diplomatic roulette, looks for the highest bidder to get his services as a negotiating partner in the high stakes of achieving Arab-Israeli peace.

Jeanne Kirkpatrick leaves her post as U.S. Ambassador to the UN where she staunchly and consistently defended Israel and is replaced by Ambassador Vernon Walters who proves to be a staunch friend of Israel as well.

PASSING THE TORCH

Israel is exhausted by its own "Vietnam quagmire and decides to withdraw its troops from Lebanon as the countries' warring factions continue their infighting.

Arab leaders descend on Washington to demand that the U.S. troops adopt a harsher policy toward Israel, which they claim is responsible for all the unrest in the Mideast.

THE BIG PUSH

At the same time, the Arabs also tell the U.S. that its support of Israel's call for direct negotiations is casting the U.S. in an anti-Arab light which can only lead to its isolation in the Mideast.

BY HOOK OR BY CROOK

Arafat tries to go it alone in his bid to convince Washington to recognize him as the sole legitimate representative of the Palestinian people, even posing as a critic of terrorist actions outside the land of Israel.

Funds to build new settlements in the West Bank are unavailable as Israel's economic crisis forces a reordering of priorities.

Reagan makes it clear that he's had it with Hussein's stonewalling regarding direct talks with Israel and continuing to cover up for the PLO, which refuses to accept UN Security Council Resolutions 242 and 338.

KOSHER INSPECTION

ETHIOPIAN JEWS

BIRTH CERTIFICATE

The Orthodox rabbinate in Israel refuses to accept the Ethiopian Jews as legitimate Jews and insists on forcing them to undergo onerous rituals before they receive the seal of approval from the Orthodox establishment.

Reagan arouses worldwide revulsion when he announces that while visiting West Germany he would pay his respects to the war dead buried in Bitburg cemetery where members of the Waffen SS are buried.

To assuage world opinion, Reagan announced that he would be even-handed and also visit the site of the Bergen-Belsen concentration camp.

Reagan's visit to Bergen-Belsen does little to mollify world anger and many note he might as well have included paying homage to earlier persecutors and killers of Jews.

Reagan's visit to Bitburg is taken as a signal by Arabs that it is appropriate to intensify their anti-Israeli pressures.

Hussein, who requires Arafat's approval to conduct peace talks, seeks to convince the U.S. that the PLO leader is not totally disgraced and discarded after his debacle in Lebanon.

In an effort to move the stalled Mideast peace talks off dead center, the U.S. tries to find some common ground with the Soviet Union by suggesting that it participate in the talks, but somehow fails to inform Israel of this move.

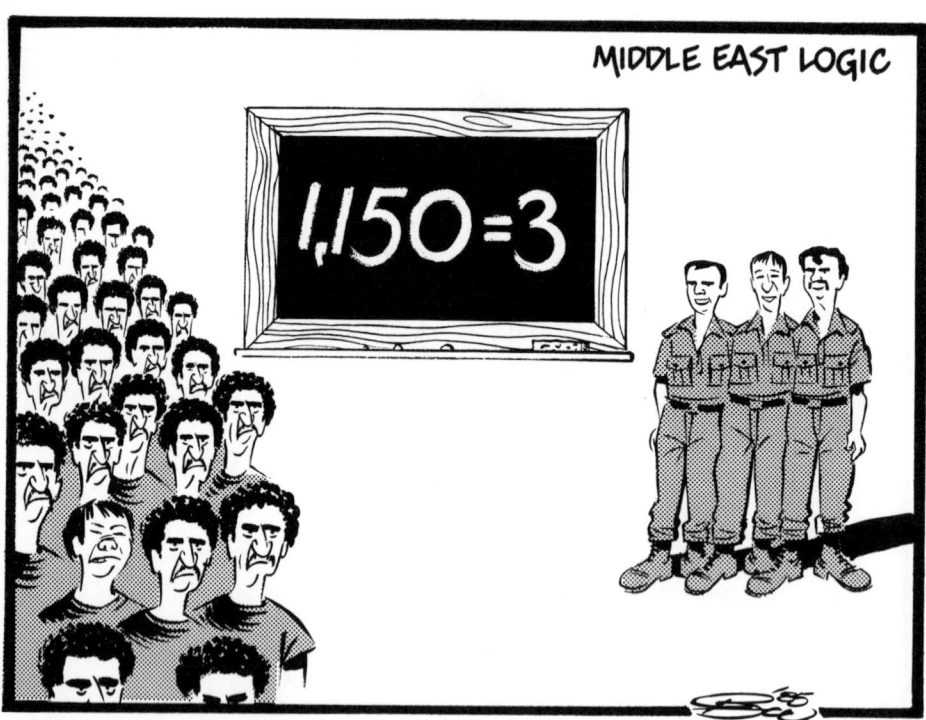

After long negotiations and pressures Israel decides to exchange 1,150 Arab prisoners for three Israeli soldiers held in captivity in Lebanon.

The extremist Shiite movement makes a daring bid for world recognition by hijacking a TWA plane in June 1985 and demanding that Israel release imprisoned terrorists before the plane's passengers are released.

Terrorism does pay off as increasing acts of violence and murder become daily news fare for television stations which outdo and outbid each other for exclusive interviews with terrorists and close-up footage of terrorist events.

Prodded by the PLO, Hussein submits a number of unexpected and unacceptable demands on Israel.

The Vatican, which has steadfastly refused to establish diplomatic relations with Israel, strains Catholic-Jewish relations when it announces a new set of guidelines regarding its attitude toward Israel.

The multi-faceted conflagration in the Mideast in which Arabs are slaughtering each other is largely ignored by the American media, which instead insists on focusing on Israel in an effort to make it the centerpiece in the ongoing tragedy.

Peres faces an awesome task trying to curb triple digit inflation and keeping Israelis from leaving for more economically more attractive countries such as the U.S.

FIGURE THIS ONE OUT

Shultz is bedeviled by the Rubik's Cube of splinter Palestinian groups, each claiming to represent the Palestinian people.

EXERCISE IN FUTILITY

The Jordanian king becomes increasingly aware that the PLO chief's intransigent stand in demanding that he represent the Palestinian contingent in peace talks is an impediment to Hussein's own willingness to move ahead on the issue of negotiations.

The Palestinian people, who have been reduced to the wretched of the earth by the Arab rulers, are not consoled by Arafat's assurances from his safe haven in Tunis, where he took refuge after fleeing Lebanon.

IT'S ONLY TABLE TENNIS

The issue of returning Taba, a sliver of beach and sand in southern Israel, to Egypt, which claims ownership becomes a bone of contention between Premier Peres and Deputy Premier Shamir. The two leaders differ about the way and how much should be returned.

BITE IT!

Austerity continued to prevail despite efforts by the Peres Administration to curb it and Israelis were admonished to bite the bullet.

Arab and Third World women attending the UN-sponsored international conference of women in Nairobi castigated Israel for allegedly denigrating the role of women and relegating them to the status of second-class citizens, but failed to address themselves to the dehumanization of women in their own countries.

THE BILL FROM DAMASCUS

Assad issues a series of demands on the U.S.A. as a ploy for the exchange of hostages held "somewhere" in Lebanon.

THOSE WHO MOURN AND THOSE WHO TURNED AWAY

ARAB LEAGUE 1945-1985

HASSAN

Arab League Conference in Casablanca broke up in disagreements between the radical states and the pro-Western states and the PLO.

Another New Year came, but peace still eludes Israel in spite of its efforts to enter into negotiations with its neighbors.

SPLIT PERSONALITY

Arafat affects different guises depending on his audience: sweetness and light to Americans, ferocious and unyielding to the Arabs. But all this has the same objective—showing to the world that he is flexible and capable of great leadership.

Israel stages a daring air strike thousands of miles from home base to bomb the PLO headquarters recently relocated to Tunisia.

LONG ARM OF JUSTICE

Italian Prime Minister Craxi genuflects toward Mecca but loses his dignity in Washington after allowing the terrorists who hijacked the Achille Lauro cruise ship and killed an American Jewish passenger, Leon Klinghoffer, to escape punishment in Italy.

British Prime Minister Thatcher is trying to build up the image of the PLO as the representative of the Palestinian people.

American media mills disregard Israel's positive achievements in industry, science, agriculture and the arts for the sake of sensationalizing.

Israel is caught in an unattainable position by the USA policy which is trying to appease the Arabs and at the same time be supportive of the Jewish State.

HAIL TO OUR HERO!

Kahane's demands that all Arabs in Israel be expelled provides Arabs with the rationale that Zionism is racism. But the founders of the Zionist movement and of the State of Israel eschewed any form of racism and strived to achieve peaceful coexistence with Arab nations and equality for the Arab inhabitants of Israel.

THIS WAS NOT THEIR GOAL
FATHERS OF ZIONISM
DEMOCRACY IS NOT FOR ISRAEL
ALL ARABS MUST LEAVE
BIBLE IS THE LAW
KAHANE
JTA©
'85

AN EASIER TARGET

Arabs find it easier and safer to defame Israel than the U.S. on which they depend for aid, but at the same time use Israel as their target to express their hostility against its sole supporter in the Mideast.

The UN has failed to fulfill its role as a world peacemaker and peace-keeper by allowing itself to be usurped by infantile Third World leftists and Arab extremists and hidebound Soviet bureaucrats.

You're 40 years old, it's time you grew up!

The professional terrorists bemoan the
fact that the Israelis are no longer in
Lebanon, so in fact, they lost the basis
for their existence.

Soviet and Arab leaders are convinced that their problems would diminish and eventually disappear if Israel did not exist. That puts them on the same wavelength.

Arab attitudes toward Israel and images of the Jewish State are determined by a maze of unconscious impressions and traits.

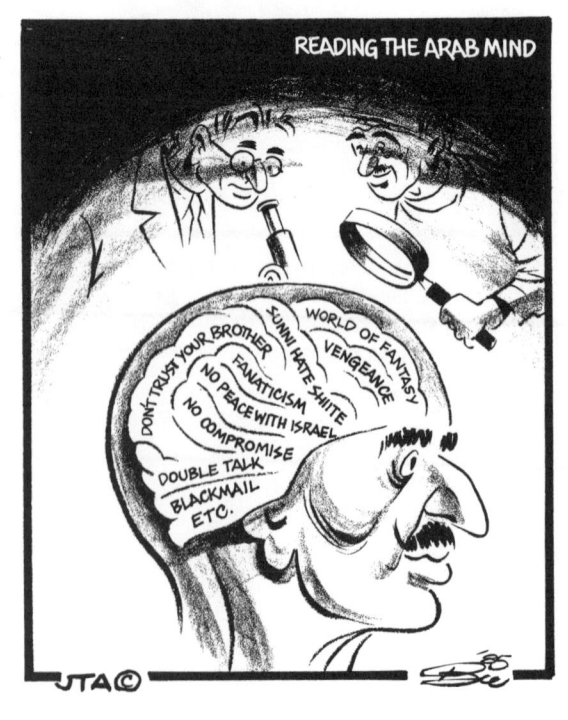

FRIENDLY EYEBALL TO EYEBALL

There are no innocents in the business of spying, and both the U.S. and Israel are equally adept at this, leading to charges and countercharges by both.

Arafat, who was used and then discarded by Hussein and then by Assad, is once again dispensable as the two Arab rulers seek to establish their own leadership of the Palestinian people.

Hints are emerging from the Kremlin that it might consider some rapprochement with Israel. Its objective is to gain a toehold in the Mideast peace process, where it can play a role if an international conference materializes.

HOW HIGH WILL IT FLY?

RENEWAL OF SOVIET-ISRAEL RELATIONS

The Peres Administration is trying desperately to curb inflation as Israelis become markedly angry and restive at the economic malaise.

I don't mind if it hurts, but don't choke me!

SHEKEL SHEKEL

111

CHANGING HAT STYLES*

*IMPRESSIONS OF RECENT TRIP TO ISRAEL

KOVA TEMBEL

For years the Israeli has been symbolized by his cap, called "Kova Tembel." As we travelled throughout the Land this year, I noticed that in many instances this has been replaced by a yarmulka.

1986

The Pollard Spy Case

Ben-Gurion Centennial

Irangate

Shamir's Return

Rise of the Ultra-Orthodox

Western Europe has been targeted for terrorist strikes by the extremist and vicious Libyan regime of Muammar Qadaffi, whose military arsenal has been stocked by the Soviet Union.

SUNRISE AT TOLEDO

RECOGNITION OF ISRAEL

WITH APOLOGIES TO EL-GRECO

An historic milestone for Israel is marked by the establishment of diplomatic relations between Spain and the Jewish State after years of behind-the-scenes negotiations.

"—Et tu Assad!"

LEBANON BLOODBATH

Assad sends troops into Lebanon's northern Bekka valley, ostensibly to help maintain law and order and quickly finds himself hip deep in the quagmire of the country's civil war.

The shadow of Britain's pre-war Foreign Minister Neville Chamberlain's sellout of Western Europe to Nazi Germany under the umbrella of appeasement casts a dark shadow as leaders of Britain, France, West Germany and Italy reject America's urgent plea for a united front against terrorism.

US AND OUR SHADOW...

"PEACE IN OUR TIME" SEPTEMBER 1938

OUR ALLIES

Anatoly Shcharansky (who has, since emigrating to Israel, changed his name to Natan Sharansky), a leading Soviet Jewish emigration activist and a leading member of the Helsinki Watch Committee, who aroused the conscience of the world after he was sentenced to 13 years in prisons and labor camps, is freed at last after years of determined campaigns for his freedom by his wife Avital and Jews and non-Jews worldwide.

The status of Taba in southern Israel continues as a contentious issue between Israel and Egypt, both of which claim ownership of the sliver of land. But Egypt is in no rush to help resolve the issue anymore than it is prepared to return its Ambassador to Israel after he was recalled when Israel invaded Lebanon. Egypt said the envoy would be returned after Israel withdrew from Lebanon, but failed to do so.

Less and less Jews were allowed to emigrate in the early 1980's, but hopes for increased emigration were raised with the emergence of Mikhail Gorbachev as the leader of the U.S.S.R.

Palestinians who seek to live in peace with Israel are forced to retreat into silence as extremist elements threaten their lives should they continue in their effort to break the cycle of violence.

ME AND MY SHADOW...

MY AUTOBIOGRAPHY — WALDHEIM

WWII NAZI SERVICE

(It took 40 years to catch up with me)

Kurt Waldheim, President of Austria and former Secretary General of the UN, is tracked down as a former member of three Nazi organizations and involved in the massacre of Yugoslav and Greek partisans and the deportation of Greek Jews to concentration camps. Waldheim continues to deny these allegations, but evidence continues to pile up to implicate him in those events.

Peres affirms that he will never negotiate with the PLO but would be willing to talk to moderate Palestinians, who are becoming harder to find.

To the world, Assad tries to appear as a temperate, logical leader, but underneath this political raiment he harbors an affinity for extremism and terrorism.

A Cleveland, Ohio auto worker, John Demjanjuk, is accused of being a former Nazi and is deported to Israel to stand trial. But many more former Nazis who entered the U.S. after World War II continue to live undetected in obscurity or evade prosecution.

THE RIGHT WEIGHT AT 38

LAST YEAR

What a difference a little dieting can do!

Continuing austerity in Israel show results. With strong economic measures the inflation went down considerably.

COOKING UP A PLOT

ISRAEL'S FREE RIDE • ANTISEMITISM • ISRAEL U.S. LIABILITY • DUAL LOYALTY

SINISTER • POLLARD CASE • FORCES

The Jonathan Pollard spy case evokes "blood libel" responses by anti-Semites and foes of Israel and high anxiety among American Jews who feel vulnerable to accusations of dual loyalty.

WHEN TWO QUARREL THE THIRD BENEFITS *(Old Polish Proverb)*

How sweet it is

Peres, whose term in office as Premier in the national unity government is about to end in a rotation agreement with Likud, hopes he can get a lease of political life as Premier as a slugfest erupts at the Herut convention between Herut leader Shamir, and his competitor for Herut leadership, David Levy. The Herut convention adjourns inconclusively and reconvenes several weeks later where Shamir is reelected.

TIME TO REMEMBER 1943-1986

ASHES OF WARSAW JEWRY

Every year Israel and Jews everywhere are reminded of the heroic uprising in the Warsaw ghetto, where the young remnants of the Jewish population stood up to the Nazi tyranny and inscribed a glorious chapter in the Jewish history.

The Reagan Administration identifies the major terrorist leaders but lacks power to stop their activities or to isolate them in the world community.

A major problem faces Israel in the growing numbers of sabras (native-born Israelis) who emigrate from the country to settle in the diaspora in the hope of finding stable economic and social conditions.

HIDE AND SEEK

The international terrorist groups are serving the interest of Soviet foreign plans. Under the disguise of liberation movements they try to disrupt the Western world.

The Mossad, Israel's secret service, finds itself implicated in the Jonathan Pollard spy case and in the deaths of two Palestinians during the course of questioning them about an Israeli bus hijacking.

Western European leaders find their countries are targets of terrorist attacks despite their willingness to tread gingerly on the issue of terrorism or to ferret out and apprehend and prosecute terrorists.

NO MORE MONKEY BUSINESS?

The Jordanian monarch finally realizes that the PLO will not modify its anti-Israeli position and its insistence that it have a separate delegation to any Mideast peace talks. Hussein severs relations with the PLO and declares himself ready to search for a road to peace through an international conference that would include the Soviet Union.

WILL THE CHEMISTRY WORK?

Peres continues his lonely efforts to find a formula suitable to create a framework for Arab-Israeli peace negotiations. A plan similar to the Marshall Plan for Western Europe after WWII a rapid but controlled industrialization, and integrated economies.

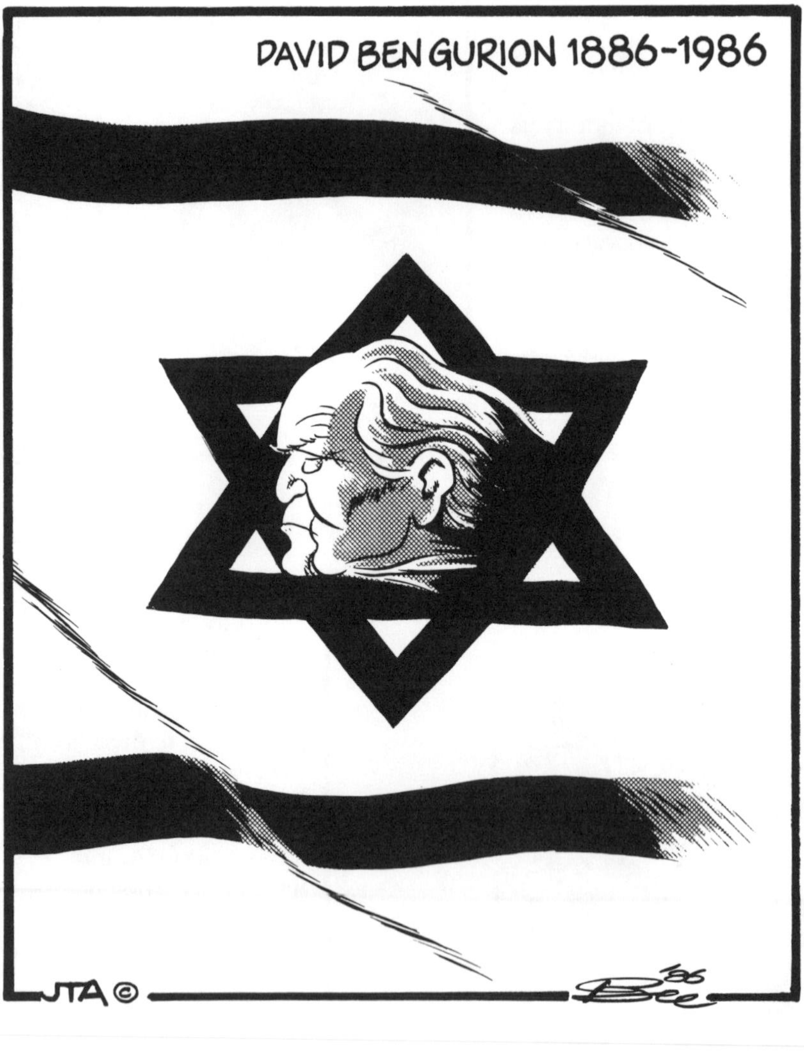
DAVID BEN GURION 1886-1986
JTA ©
'86
Bee

> From David
> to David
> there was none
> like David

Israel and the Jewish world celebrated the 100th anniversary of the Father of the Jewish State. Called the George Washington of Israel, Ben Gurion led the nation through the most difficult time and carried it to its independence. His vision shaped the foundation of the State, though his greatest hope of development of the Negev is yet unfulfilled.

It is a known fact that every nation spies on each other, but because Jay Pollard was caught red-handed, the investigation of the Justice Department focused on Israel.

The tensions and violence between Orthodox and secular Jews in Israel continues relentlessly and threatens to split the Jewish State.

King Hassan of Morocco invites Israeli Premier Peres to visit the Arab kingdom and both are aware that the PLO is fomenting dissatisfaction among Palestinians about Hassan's move.

As a result of Peres' visit to Morocco, contradicting impressions are being drawn by both sides.

A Soviet and Israeli delegation meet in Helsinki, the first such formal public meeting since the USSR broke diplomatic relations with Israel in 1967. The ostensible agenda of dealing with Soviet property in Israel provides a possible basis for further talks about a diplomatic rapprochement.

The investigation into Shin Beth's mishandling of Arab prisoners pointed at a possible responsibility for the death of the two captured bus hijackers plagues the office of Prime Minister Shamir.

The U.S. supports an Israeli plan for the economic development of the West Bank as a way of improving the living standards of the Palestinians there and simultaneously dissipating discontent which serves as a breeding ground for extremists.

THE SOWER
(after Millet)

Israel embarks on a series of economic and diplomatic ventures in Africa to aid the developing nations cope with famine, drought, hunger, disease and illiteracy and to lay the basis for the resumption of relations with those countries that had broken ties during the 1973 Yom Kippur War.

It's close to election time again and Presidential hopefuls, including Vice President George Bush, log hundreds of miles in the Mideast to use as evidence of their unceasing efforts to create amity between Israel and its Arab neighbors.

PASSING THE BALL

DIPLOMATIC INITIATIVES

Peres prepares to rotate office with Shamir and takes the opportunity to remind the Israeli public that he has chalked up some formidable successes which Shamir should follow up.

Israel notifies the Soviet Union that it is prepared to resume diplomatic relations that go beyond non-essential or secondary issues.

The killing of Jews by Arab extremists as happened in Istanbul is only a prelude to terrorist attacks on the rest of the world. The lesson begins to sink in that the elimination of terrorism is everybody's business.

Picking an Ambassador to the U.S. is not always done logically in Israel. Most often it is a game of Israeli roulette, a political payoff which sometimes backfires.

Years go by and Israel is still waiting for a chance to sit down with its Arab neighbors and talk peace. With the exception of Egypt, this goal remains elusive.

After the rotation of Premiership from Peres to Shamir, the Likud leader seeks to induce harmony in the ranks of his Likud colleagues.

Britain broke off relations with Syria after a Syrian diplomat was implicated in an attempt by an Arab terrorist to blow up an Israeli El-Al plane.

A news item in a Lebanese magazine broke the story that the Reagan Administration is trying to negotiate with Iran about the release of the American hostages.

Premier Jacques Chirac of France issues a passionate defense of Syrian President Assad, portraying him as a victim of a secret Israeli plot to blame him for terrorist actions against French peace contingents stationed in Lebanon.

Mordechai Vanunu, an Israeli nuclear technician, provided secret information about Israel's nuclear complex in Dimona to a newspaper in London. He was traced to London and then to Italy and Cyprus by Israeli agents assigned to his case and returned to Israel to stand trial.

Both the American and Israeli political establishments found themselves in another international mess when they fell prey to speculation that moderate Iranians were mobilizing forces to topple the Ayatollah Khomeini.

Reagan, who had repeatedly affirmed that he would eschew any deals with terrorists, delights three heavies—Assad, Qadaffi and Arafat—when members of his Administration are found to have approved arms shipments to Iran.

The Orthodox establishment in Israel receives a setback when the Supreme Court rules that conversions performed by Conservative and Reform rabbis are legitimate.

Khomeini, caught in a political indiscretion when he secretly agrees to accept military hardware from Israeli arms merchants, steps up his anti-Israeli and anti-Zionist attacks to appease his critics.

THE SACRIFICIAL LAMB

The Reagan Administration, embarrassed over its own arms deal with Iran, blames Israel for pressuring it to do so and even acting as a middleman in the transactions.

> **WHO'S TO BLAME?**
>
> "I knew nothing about it – it was a third country!"

Reagan himself, however, is careful not to openly identify Israel as the country that acted in concert with the U.S. in the Iran arms deal, but his allusion is loud an clear.

1987

Peres-Shamir Tug-o-War

Soviet's Peek-a-Boo

Lavi's Downfall

Waiting for Hussein

American Jews and Israel

Premier Shamir, on a visit to Washington, has come to grips with a host of international problems involving U.S.-Israel relations which had been severely strained during the year.

THE SHADOW HE LEAVES BEHIND

Shamir's visit to Washington is a definite diplomatic success as the tensions that preceded his visit are diminished after his meetings with Administration officials.

MISS AND HIT

Israel prepares itself from some political and diplomatic bruises as disclosures unfold that the U.S. availed itself of Israeli aid in fighting the Sandinistas by arming the Contras.

SALESMANSHIP... SOVIET STYLE

The Soviet Union is eager to participate in Mideast peace negotiations, but its credentials hardly qualify it to act as an honest broker.

Demjanjuk, alleged to be "Ivan the Terrible" by concentration camp inmates whom he tortured while he was a Nazi prison guard, denies the allegation and insists that he is a victim of mistaken identity and knows nothing about the crimes attributed to him.

WILL THE REAL IVAN STAND UP

SCAPEGOAT TRAP

More and more facts point to the story that Israeli leadership was heavily involved in the negotiations between Washington and the Iranian "moderates" in the arms deal called "Irangate."

NEW POSTER IN RUMANIA

Israel has sought to stem the tide of Soviet Jews going to countries other than Israel after they receive exit visas. One Israeli plan calls for direct Moscow-Tel Aviv flights through Rumania rather than through Austria or Italy, where many Jews decide to "drop out."

The ghost of Arafat's past continues to hover over the political landscape despite his waning influence among Arabs and Palestinians. His apparition is periodically buoyed by the willingness of Western governments and the Soviet Union to inflate and then exaggerate his importance.

ANOTHER RESURRECTION

Premier Shamir and Foreign Minister Peres have contrary approaches to the form and substance of peace negotiations. But both are hobbled in their efforts to pursue their respective proposals by the nature of the national unity government which requires agreement by both partners.

– PARDON ME!
ISRAEL
AMERICAN JEWRY
POLLARD FALLOUT JUICE
UTA ©
'87

A TRAGIC SLIP

American Jews react with trepidation that the Pollard spy case in which Israel is implicated will evoke the traditional anti-Israel and anti-Semitic canard of dual loyalty. Israel is also caught in a delicate diplomatic situation and tries to explain away any relationship with Pollard by insisting that he acted alone. But the Pollard affair engulfs Israel as the U.S. demands that Israel's role be carefully scrutinized. Israeli leaders find themselves trapped in a maze of domestic criticism for having mishandled the entire episode while establishment American Jewish leaders criticize Israel for compromising their relations with the Administration and the public.

IT TOOK A STRONG ARM

25,000 NAMES OF SUSPECTED NAZIS

WALDHEIM AND ALIKE

NETANYAHU

Israel's Ambassador to the UN, Binyamin Netanyahu, demands that the UN war crimes commission files, mouldering in an office building and unavailable for inspection, be opened to public scrutiny. Many of those identified in the files are still alive and some are living in safety and obscurity in the U.S., Canada, England and other Western countries.

Reagan finds himself off the hook—for a while—as Congressional committees investigating the Irangate scandal are told by some of the behind-the-scenes arms dealers that Israel played an important role in the affair.

The Cabinet meets in closed session to formulate a policy statement on the Pollard case and then announces that the government knew nothing about the caper. But this disclaimer is not readily accepted as credible by many Israelis.

The Saudis lead the Arab boycott of Israel but find nevertheless that they are not successful in isolating Israel in the world market.

The hidebound Orthodox leadership suffers a setback when the Knesset rejects a bid by the Orthodox Shas Party to amend the Law of Return to include a clause that conversions to Judaism are not legitimate unless they are performed according to halacha (Jewish law). The Knesset also voted to accept as legitimate conversions performed by Reform and Conservative rabbis.

American support of an international peace conference on the Mideast is greeted with suspicion and disdain by Assad, who is hoping for a military confrontation with Israel sometime in the future.

The darling of American Jews, Abba Eban finds very little support in Israel for his policies which are based on the early partition plans.

The Soviet Union continues to maintain a safe diplomatic distance from Israel but tests the possibility of renewing some form of relations, even if it is limited temporarily to inspecting Soviet property in Israel and making contact with Russian nationals.

The Reagan Administration becomes convinced that the terrorist PLO is not a legitimate diplomatic representative and moves to close its office in Washington. The move follows mounting pressure from the organized Jewish community and legislators who campaigned for an international quarantine of the terrorist group.

The USSR, a world leader in the development of nuclear weapons, warns Israel against developing nuclear capacity for military use.

Saudi Arabia, led by slick politicians, realizes that Israel is the only gainer in the ongoing warfare between Arab states and Arab factions and calls for an end to the internecine warfare and for a united front against Israel.

Shamir continues to be adamantly opposed to an international conference on Mideast peace as proposed by Peres. Shamir warns that Peres' effort courts disaster for Israel by providing a back door for Russians and Palestinians who are members of the PLO to participate in the negotiations.

More Soviet bloc countries take steps to establish consular, cultural and scientific relations with Israel, a move Sovietologists observe could not be made without Kremlin approval. This development also appears to bode well for increased Soviet Jewish emigration and for greater freedom for Soviet Jews who do not emigrate.

STRINGS ATTACHED

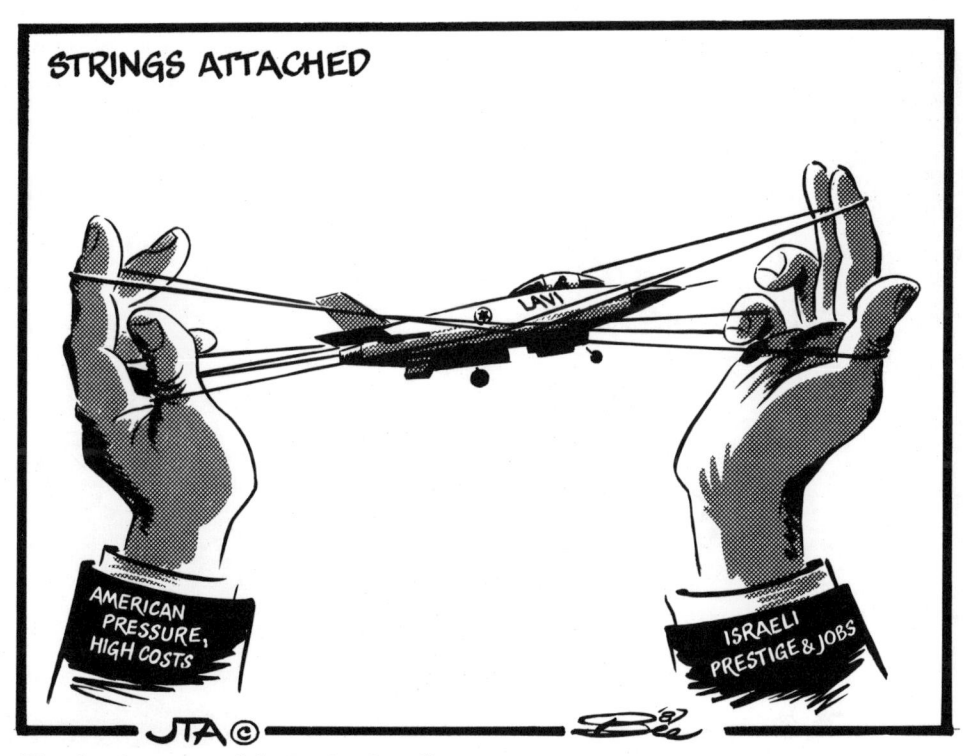

AMERICAN PRESSURE, HIGH COSTS

LAVI

ISRAELI PRESTIGE & JOBS

The development of the Lavi as Israel's second-generation jet fighter becomes doubtful as the U.S. claims that it is too costly to produce it and some in Israel agree. However, Israeli leaders claim that the production of the Lavi is a military necessity and that, in addition, it would create more jobs for Israelis and Americans and would not be as expensive to construct as the U.S. claims.

Israel is prepared to discuss diplomatic relations with the Soviet Union and its participation in an international conference on Mideast peace if it takes a positive stand on a number of issues of vital concern to Israel and world Jewry. Israel is forthcoming in its demands on behalf of Soviet Jewry, but the Russians have not yet adopted a policy of "perestroyka" on this issue.

A PEACEFUL SABBATH IN JERUSALEM

The ultra-Orthodox use violence against secular Jews to keep them from violating the sanctity of the Sabbath. The ultras campaign to keep the cinemas closed on Friday nights and thoroughfares clear of moving vehicles Friday nights and Saturdays. They refuse to acknowledge that their violence against secular Jews, which frequently results in injuries, is itself a desecration of the Sabbath.

Pope John Paul II exercises his prerogative to refuse to establish diplomatic ties with Israel, thereby angering world Jewry and creating tensions in Catholic-Jewish relations.

The Russians keep Israelis guessing about their intentions by using the oldie but goodies carrot and stick method of diplomacy.

The "angel" of Soviet Jewish Prisoners of Conscience, Ida Nudel, is finally allowed to leave the Soviet Union after years of suffering in prison, labor camps and internal exile. This heroic fighter for Jewish emigration rights, who won the support and respect of Jews and non-Jews around the world, immigrated to Israel, where she continues to campaign for the right of other Soviet Jews to emigrate.

Shultz returns to the Mideast to examine the ailing and sluggish peace process, but his patients seem to be allergic to his prescriptions for moving the peace process off dead center.

Palestinians who respond to American urgings that they renounce violence against Israel and help the peace process to move ahead are either frightened into silence or killed by PLO extremists.

Differences about an International Peace Conference prompted many American Jews to side with Foreign Minister Peres and not with Prime Minister Shamir, who opposed a conference with the participation of the Soviet Union that does not have diplomatic relations with the Jewish State.

Prime Minister Shamir, who opposes an international peace conference, would prefer individual negotiations with each of its Arab neighbors.

The controversial and anti-Israeli Secretary of UNESCO was finally forced out of office after years of mishandling the agency.

Israeli President Chaim Herzog paid an official visit to the United States, spoke before a full session of the Congress and paid a visit to President Reagan. The Irish-born Herzog was elected to his second five-year term as the "Chief of State."

At long last the UN War Crimes Commission files are opened to diplomats, historians, researchers and journalists. It is expected that many war criminals, living in obscurity and safety in many Western countries, including the U.S., will be publicly identified and will be prosecuted for their crimes against humanity.

The Arab Summit met in Amman with the participation of Egypt which was excluded from this body ever since signing the Camp David agreement with Israel. The top item on the agenda was the war between Iraq and Iran while the Palestinian question was relegated to the very last.

A TREE GROWS IN GAZA

Riots exploded in Gaza after a traffic accident when four Arabs were killed by an Israeli truck. Soon the rioting spread to the West Bank. Nearly 100 Palestinians died in stone throwing and Molotov cocktail confrontation with the Israeli Army.

As the riots continued, Israel had to apply a strong arm policy to deal with the spreading unrest. While in the U.N., a one sided resolution was passed unanimously condemning the Israeli way of handling the situation.

1988

Crackdown on Riots

Gaza and West Bank

Israel's 40th Anniversary

Israel had to make hard decisions as it was confronted with the wide spread of the uprising. For a country that is proud of its democracy and high ethics, it is hard to adopt a policy of beating and breaking the bones of the Palestinian stone throwers.

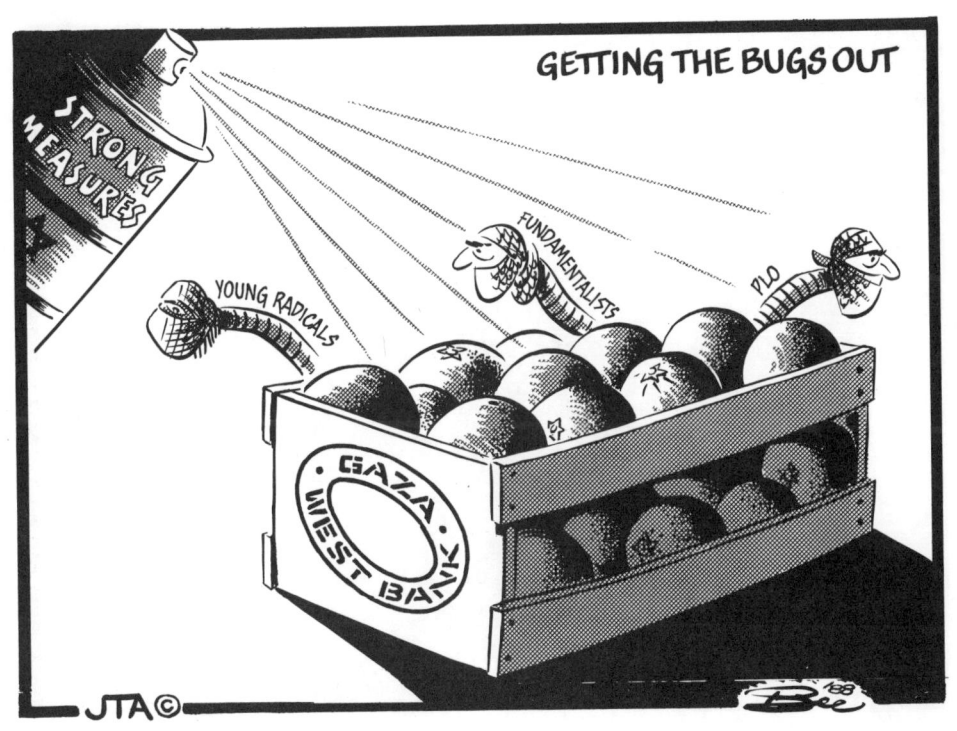

As an effective means to gain control over the situation, Israeli security forces rounded up the suspected rioters and the instigators, jailed them and singled out nine for deportation.

Pictures and reports coming out of the territories angered many American-Jewish leaders and they called on Israeli leaders to change their policy which they contend went against the grain of Jewish teachings.

President Hosni Mubarak during his official visit to Washington, suggested a six-month cooling off period on the West Bank and the Gaza Strip. He told President Reagan that Egypt is determined to serve as a channel of communication between Israel and the Arab world.

Jordan's King Hussein continued to make the rounds of European capitals, pushing his own version of an international peace conference. At the same time, he vacillated on the role of the PLO, verbally embracing Arafat one day and rejecting him the next. He has officially spoken to everyone but the Israelis.

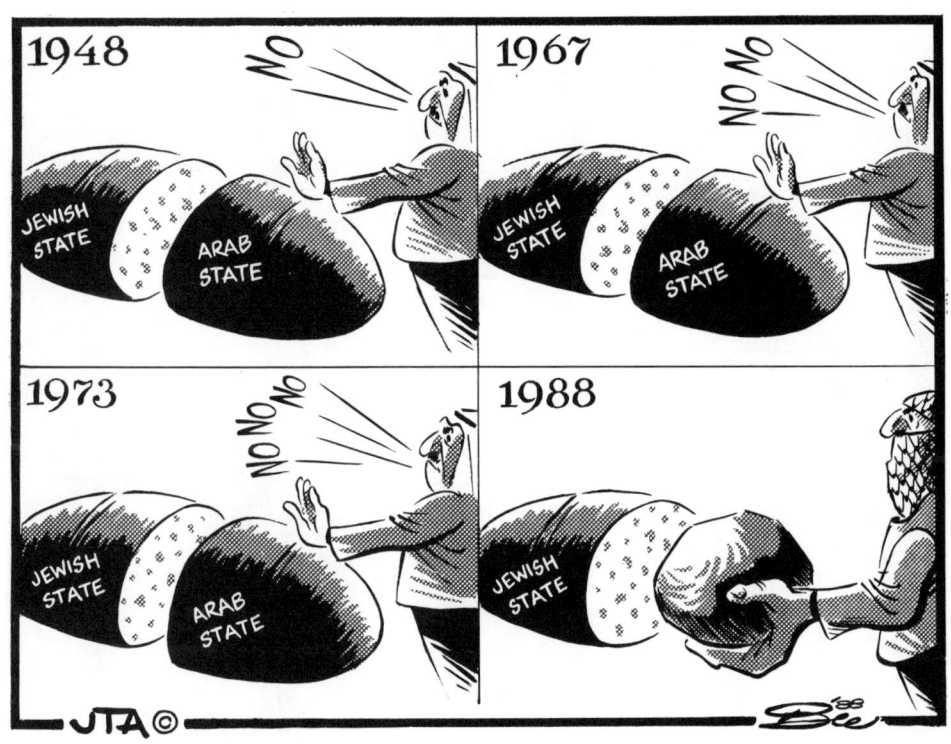

For 40 years the Arab states have rejected all proposals put forth by the United Nations and the State of Israel. Their intransigence has resulted in the unrest in the territories, where the Arabs kept the refugee camps festering for four decades.

LIGHTS! CAMERA! ACTION!

And one of the longest-lasting television mini-series comes to the screen. "Death in Gaza" has focused on Israeli efforts to quell the disorder. No mention or pictures of the nearly 300 members of the Israel Defense Forces maimed (some of them permanently) by the well-planned attacks of stone-throwing teenagers urged on by Moslem fundamentalists and the PLO. Henry Kissinger's advice to Israel: ban TV cameras and photographers from the scene.

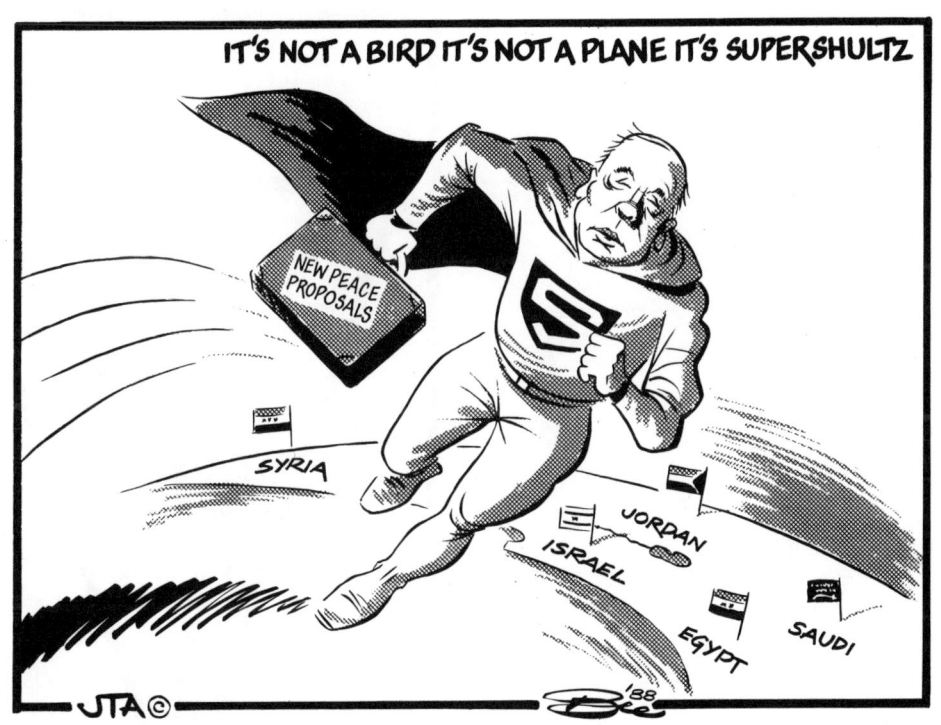

The American Secretary of State, trying to move stalled peace efforts off dead center and to bring an end to the riots in the West Bank and Gaza, logged 21,416 miles in 10 days of shuttle diplomacy between Israelis and Arabs and between Shamir and Peres.

Ancient times

From time immemorial Israel has been caught in a squeeze. This simple analogy of the history of the Jewish people added up to the facts that in spite of its tragic circumstances, it is the land and history that binds the destiny of its people.

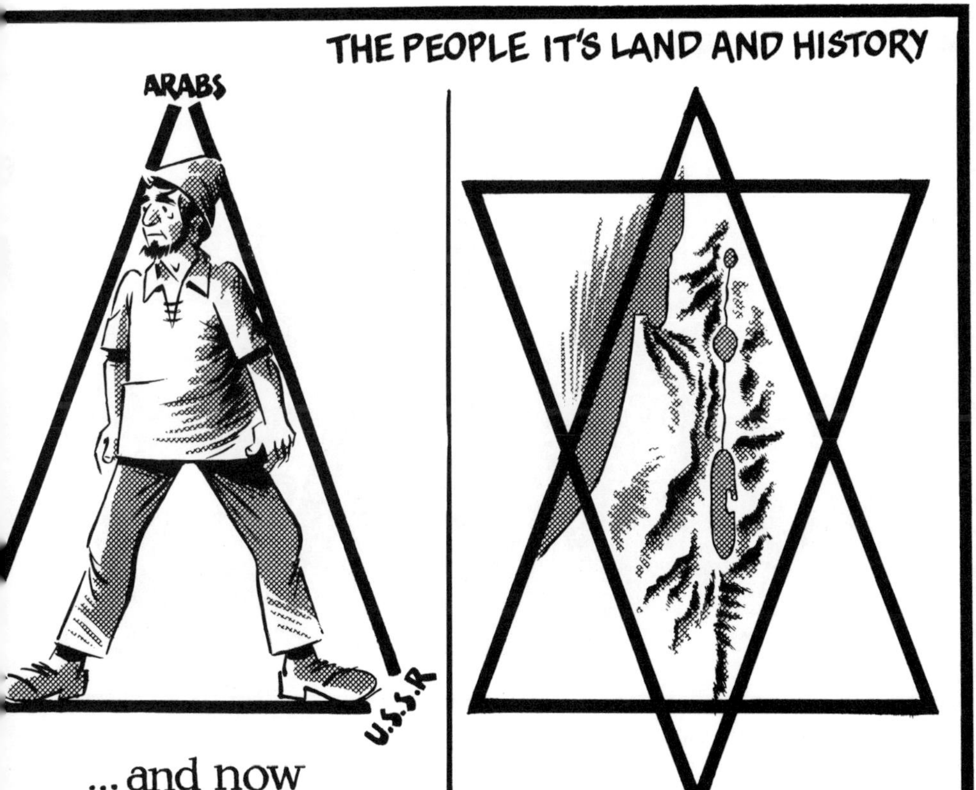
THE PEOPLE IT'S LAND AND HISTORY
ARABS
U.S.S.R
... and now
'88

MOTHER OF TERROR

Yasir Arafat publicly bemoaned the fact that the PLO was not given enough "credit" for their role in the uprising in the territories. PLO responded to Shultz' peace effort with a bomb plot on his life and the bloody hijacking of a civilian bus near Beersheva.

Middle East observers wondered whether the United States had enough muscle to pressure the Arabs and the Israelis to accept the Shultz peace plan. The Secretary of State acknowledged the weight of the obstacles that he has to overcome.

> **PASSOVER 1988**
>
> "We survived the desert for 40 years, but you made the desert bloom in 40 years. Make sure and keep it!"

Every year at this time the Jewish people are reminded that each one has to regard himself as though he had personally come out of slavery. As it is said, "The Holy One took us out from Egypt in order to bring us hither, to give us the land which he had sworn unto our fathers."

It has been a hard climb with many accomplishments, triumphs, trials and errors. Someday Israel will reach the top step and find peace and tranquility. In the meantime Mazel Tov on this milestone anniversary!